Barnyard Buddies
In the Chicken Coop

by Patricia M. Stockland
illustrated by Todd Ouren

Special thanks to content consultant:
Roger Stockland, Farmer/Rancher
B.S. Agricultural Engineering, South Dakota State University

visit us at
www.abdopublishing.com

Published by Magic Wagon, a division of the ABDO Publishing
Group, 8000 West 78th Street, Edina, Minnesota 55439.

Printed in the United States.

Text by Patricia M. Stockland
Illustrations by Todd Ouren
Edited by Jill Sherman
Interior layout and design by Todd Ouren
Cover design by Todd Ouren

Library of Congress Cataloging-in-Publication Data
Stockland, Patricia M.
In the chicken coop / Patricia M. Stockland ; illustrated by Todd Ouren ; content
consultant , Roger Stockland.
        p.cm. – (Barnyard buddies)
Includes index.
ISBN 978-1-60270-023-9
1. Chickens—Juvenile literature. I. Ouren, Todd. II. Stockland, Roger. III. Title. IV.
Series.
SF487.5.S75 2008
636.5—dc22
                                                    2007004689

As the sun comes up, the rooster crows.

Cock-a-doodle-doo!

It is time for the chickens to wake up.

A rooster is a male chicken.
Sometimes a rooster is called a cock.

The hens leave their roosts. They peck the
ground for food.

Yum! Cracked corn.

Yum! A beetle!

Farmers feed chickens ground corn. Chickens also eat bugs, grain, fruit, and seeds.

5

Some of the hens go sit in nests. They will lay eggs in the nests. Some hens stay and sit on their eggs to keep them warm.

Eggs must be kept warm. This is
where baby chickens come from.

Not all eggs will hatch a chick. The farmer takes away some eggs. These are the eggs you eat.

Farmers raise chickens
for eggs and meat.

What is that noise? An eggshell cracks. Soon a **cheep cheep** is heard. A chick hatches from its shell.

Chicks are baby chickens.

The chick is wet. Soon the chick dries. Its soft down is fluffy and yellow. The chick follows its mother.

Chicks are covered in
feathers called "down."

The hens in the yard spend most of the day pecking for food. They scratch the ground. They peck, peck, **peck.**

Hens use their claws to scratch the
ground. Claws are sharp nails.

15

The chicks learn to hunt for food. They follow the hens and peck the ground.

Chicks do not drink milk. They eat corn
and bugs just like adult chickens.

The rooster stretches his wings and crows.
Roosters crow to show they are the bosses.

Roosters crow throughout the day,
not just in the morning.

19

It is time for the chickens to go to bed. Each chicken finds its roost.

Cock-a-doodle-doo!

Chicken Diagram

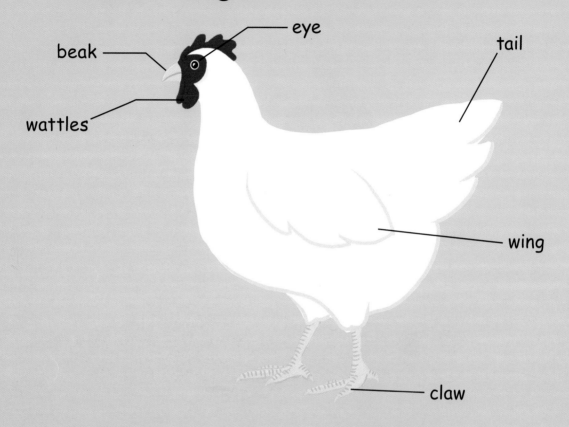

beak

eye

tail

wattles

wing

claw

Glossary

claws—sharp nails.
cock—a rooster.
down—tiny feathers that keep a young bird warm.
roost—a place where birds go to sleep at night.

Fun Facts

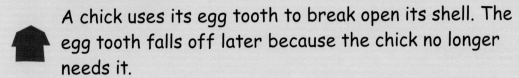

A chick uses its egg tooth to break open its shell. The egg tooth falls off later because the chick no longer needs it.

Chickens clean their feathers by taking dust baths. The dirt and dust keep their feathers dry and get rid of bugs.

Chickens can fly, but not very far. The longest known flight was just over 300 feet (91 m).

Chickens will eat small pieces of sharp stone to help them digest food.

In a flock, chickens create a pecking order. The strongest chickens rank at the top. The weaker chickens are at the bottom.

There are many different types, or breeds, of chickens. Breeds vary in size and color.

A rooster will sit on a high perch to keep lookout for predators and guard his hens.

Index